THE ELEMENTS

Bromine

Krista West

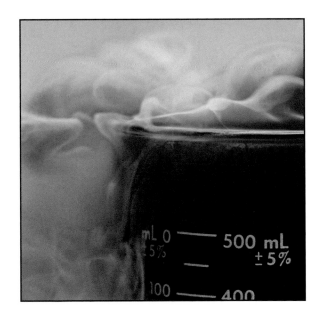

Marshall Cavendish
Benchmark

New York

Marshall Cavendish Benchmark
99 White Plains Road
Tarrytown, New York 10591

www.marshallcavendish.us

Library of Congress Cataloging-in-Publication Data

West, Krista,
Bromine / Krista West.
p.   cm – (The elements)
Includes index.
ISBN 978-0-7614-2685-1
1. Bromine. 2. Bromine compounds. I. Title. II. Series.

QD181.B7W47 2007
546'.733--dc22

2006051812

1 6 5 4 3 2

Printed in Malaysia

Picture credits
Front cover: Corbis
Back cover: Shutterstock

Corbis: Stephanie Calrera/Zefa 13, Kit Kittle 26b, Wally McNamee 23,
Nathan Benn 3, 17, Richard T. Nowitz 11, Kevin Schafer 16
Corbis Sygma: Yves Forester 5
Mary Evans Picture Library: 14
Photos.com: 10
2006 RGB Research Ltd: www.element-collection.com 8
Shutterstock: Elena Elisseera 6, Ivan Josifovic 26t, Ana Vasileva 22b
Science Photo Library: Andrew Lambert Photography 19, 25, Victor De Schwanberg 22t,
Science Source 27, Charles D. Winters 1, 9, 18, 30
Tosoh Corporation: 4
University of Pennsylvania Library: Edgar Fahs Smith Collection 15

Series created by The Brown Reference Group plc.
Designed by Sarah Williams
www.brownreference.com

Contents

What is bromine?

Where can you find bromine? Take a swim in the ocean or build a sand castle and you will be covered in atoms of this unusual element. An atom is the smallest piece of an element that still acts like that element.

Many of the salty substances in seawater contain bromine. In these salts, atoms of bromine are bound to atoms of other elements. When atoms of two or more elements join together, they form a compound. Compounds are produced by chemical reactions.

Reactive liquid

Bromine is a reactive element and forms compounds with atoms of other elements very easily. Because its atoms form compounds so easily, pure bromine is never found in nature. Bromine is only ever purified by people.

Pure bromine is one of only two elements that are a liquid at room temperature. The other is mercury, a shiny, silver-colored metal. Bromine is the only liquid nonmetal. The liquid is reddish brown, has a strong smell, and is very poisonous.

Uses of bromine

Humans take advantage of this unusual element in many ways. In the past, a bromine compound was added to gasoline. Today, bromine is used in many products, including televisions and computers. The bromine compounds reduce the chances that those things will catch on fire.

Bromine is a dark red-brown liquid in normal conditions. It is the only nonmetal element that is a liquid when it is in its pure form.

Bromine can also be used in citrus-flavored soft drinks, to clean water, to poison pests, and to produce old-fashioned photographs. Many people might not know much about bromine, but tiny amounts of this element are all around us.

A firefighting plane drops bromine compounds over a wildfire. The bromine will stop the trees from burning. The main use of bromine is in fireproofing material.

The bromine atom

Everything in the universe is made up of atoms. Think of an atom as an ingredient in a recipe. Ingredients are combined to make a certain dish. Compounds contain a combination of atoms of different elements. Each compound has set numbers and types of atoms in it.

All of the atoms of an element have the same structure. The structure of an element's atoms determines how and when they will combine with the atoms of other elements.

The center of the atom contains a tiny ball of particles called the nucleus. The nucleus holds two types of particles: protons and neutrons. Protons have a positive charge, while neutrons have no charge

The water in swimming pools is kept clean with chemicals that include bromine compounds. The bromine kills dangerous bacteria that might make swimmers ill.

at all—they are neutral. Particles called electrons, which have a negative charge, surround the nucleus in layers, or shells.

The atoms of each element have different numbers of protons, neutrons, and electrons inside. The number of protons in an atom is called the atomic number. Bromine has 35 protons, so its atomic number is 35. No other element has this number of protons. Atoms have the same number of electrons and protons, so bromine atoms also have 35 electrons.

The other number used to describe atoms is the atomic mass number. This is the number of all protons plus neutrons in the nucleus of an atom.

When the nuclei of bromine atoms are looked at together, some have 44 neutrons and others have 46 neutrons. The average number of neutrons in a bromine atom is 44.9. So the element's atomic mass number is 79.9 (44.9 + 35). This is generally rounded up to 80.

Bromine bonds

The number of electrons in the bromine atom's outer shell determines how the atom bonds with another atom. A bond is formed when two atoms give, take, or

BROMINE ATOM

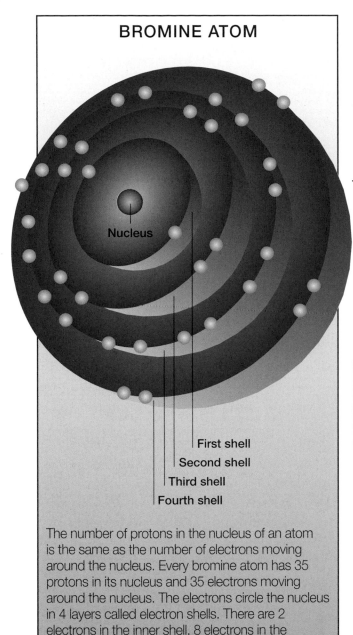

Nucleus

First shell
Second shell
Third shell
Fourth shell

The number of protons in the nucleus of an atom is the same as the number of electrons moving around the nucleus. Every bromine atom has 35 protons in its nucleus and 35 electrons moving around the nucleus. The electrons circle the nucleus in 4 layers called electron shells. There are 2 electrons in the inner shell, 8 electrons in the second shell, 18 electrons in the third shell, and 7 electrons in the fourth shell.

Most atoms form bonds so that the outer electron shell will be full. Having a full outer shell makes the atom very stable. Bromine's outer shell can hold a maximum of eight electrons. A bromine atom has seven electrons in its outer shell. It needs just one more to become stable. Bromine atoms form bonds by either taking an electron from another atom, or by sharing an electron with another atom.

Because they need only one electron, bromine atoms pull on the electrons of other atoms strongly. Atoms that require

share some of their electrons. The two atoms then become connected to each other, making a compound. When two or more atoms bond together, they form a structure called a molecule.

more electrons to fill their shells pull on electrons of other atoms more weakly. As a result, bromine reacts more easily than most other elements.

One of a group

Elements with the same number of electrons in the outer shells of their atoms will form bonds in the same way. Chemists arrange these elements into groups. Bromine belongs to a group called the halogens. All halogens have seven outer electrons. The other halogen elements are fluorine, chlorine, iodine, and astatine.

Bromine floats on mercury in a test tube. Bromine is less dense than mercury but more dense than water. A cup of bromine weighs about three times more than a cup of water.

ATOMS AT WORK

Bromine atoms (Br) have seven electrons in the outermost electron shell. To become stable, bromine needs one more electron to fill its shell.

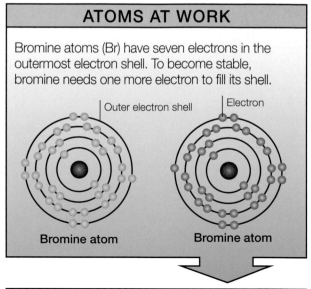

Two bromine atoms share one electron so that they both have eight electrons in the outermost electron shell. This sharing means that the atoms are held together by a covalent bond. The atoms form a bromine molecule (Br_2).

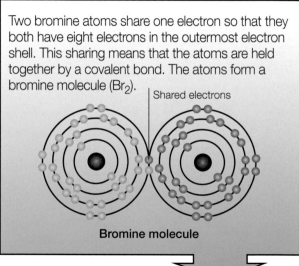

Bromine molecule

Pure bromine is made up of bromine molecules.

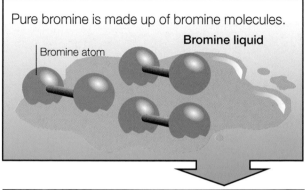

The reaction that takes place can be written like this:

Br + Br → Br$_2$

Special characteristics

Bromine liquid turns into a gas easily. The gas, or vapor, is red-brown, like liquid bromine. Bromine vapor is heavier than air and sinks to the floor.

All substances can exist in three forms: solid, gas, or liquid. These three forms are called states of matter. At normal room temperature, most elements exist as a solid or gas. In a solid, the atoms or molecules are packed tightly together to form a hard substance with a fixed shape. For example, gold and carbon are solids at room temperature. In a gas, the atoms or molecules are all completely separate from each other and move around in all directions. Because of this a gas has no fixed shape and spreads out to fill any space. Oxygen and hydrogen are gases at room temperature.

Bromine is a liquid at room temperature. In a liquid, the atoms or molecules are bound loosely. The atoms do not separate but they can flow past each other. As a result, liquids have no fixed shape. Instead they take the shape of their container.

BROMINE FACTS

- Chemical symbol: Br
- Atomic number: 35
- Atomic mass number: 80
- Melting point: 19 °F (–7.3 °C)
- Boiling point: 137.8 °F (58.8 °C)
- Density: 3.11 grams per cubic cm. (3.11 times the density of water.)

Sight and smell

Although bromine is a liquid, it easily turns into a gas. Bromine gas smells like chlorine, the chemical often used to keep swimming pools clean. However, the smell of bromine is much stronger. The name *bromine* comes from the Greek word *bromos*, meaning "bad smell." The element's color is also distinctive—it is a dark red-brown.

Bromine is dangerous to humans in all forms because it damages parts of the body. When breathed as a gas (even in small amounts), it can seriously damage the lungs and throat. When it touches the skin, it causes painful blisters and burns.

Bromine in nature

Bromine is never found as a pure element in nature. The element is so reactive and ready to form bonds that it is always bonded to other atoms forming compounds. Natural compounds are called minerals. Bromine minerals occur in small amounts in rocks and soil and in larger amounts in the oceans.

Bromine in rocks

Earth's outermost layer of rock is called the crust. It contains several bromine compounds. Scientists estimate that two parts per million (ppm) of Earth's rocks is bromine. That means in a sample of one million pieces of Earth's crust, only two of them would be pieces of bromine. Compared to other elements, that makes bromine relatively rare in rocks.

Most of the time, bromine binds with other elements to form salts. A salt is a compound that forms when one atom gives away electrons, and another atom adds electrons to its outer shell.

When an atom gains an electron, the atom becomes negatively charged. This is because the atom now has more

Bromine compounds—or salts—in rocks are washed away by waterfalls, rivers, and springs. The water then carries the salts into the ocean.

DID YOU KNOW?

THE DEAD SEA

The Dead Sea is a large lake in the desert between Israel and Jordan. It has one of the largest concentrations of bromine compounds on the planet. Unlike ordinary seawater, which contains about 85 ppm bromine, the Dead Sea has up to 5,000 ppm bromine. Much of this bromine is contained in bromide salts. The Dead Sea is at the bottom of a steep valley below the level of the oceans. Over the years, the sea's water has been evaporated away, leaving behind the bromides dissolved in it. The salts are very concentrated, and the large amount of salt makes the Dead Sea's water very dense (packed with many atoms). As a result, people float in it, like wood floats on normal water.

negatively-charged electrons than positively-charged protons. An atom with any charge is called an ion. During a reaction, a bromine atom gains one electron to fill its outer shell. By doing this the atom forms a negative ion (Br^-), also called a bromide ion. The other atom loses

A tourist at the Dead Sea floats in the salty water. It is the large amount of salts, including bromine compounds, that make it easy to float in the water.

ATOMS AT WORK

A bromine atom needs one electron to complete its outermost electron shell and become stable. A sodium atom needs to lose one electron to become stable.

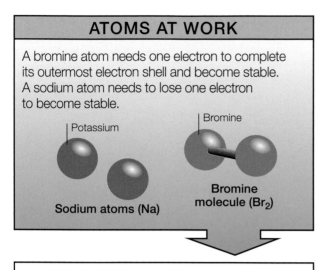

Sodium atoms (Na)

Bromine molecule (Br$_2$)

The bromine molecule splits into atoms, and the sodium atoms give an electron to each of the bromine atoms. All atoms become ions. The sodium ions (Na$^+$) have a positive charge. The bromide ions (Br$^-$) have a negative charge.

Sodium atom | Electron | Bromine atom

Sodium ion | Bromide ion

The opposite charges make the ions attract each other, creating a bond between them. The two ions form a molecule of sodium bromide (KBr).

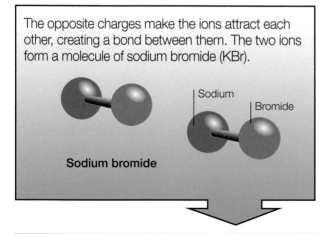

Sodium bromide

Sodium | Bromide

The reaction that takes place can be written like this:

$$2Na + Br_2 \rightarrow 2NaBr$$

an electron to become stable. This is now a positively-charged ion. For example, sodium (Na) loses one electron to become an Na$^+$ ion. Opposite charges attract each other, so the bromide ion is pulled toward the sodium ion. The attraction creates a bond that holds the two ions together forming sodium bromide (NaBr).

Sodium bromide and potassium bromide (KBr) are two of the most common bromine compounds. On land, most of these compounds are in rocks buried deep underground.

Bromine in the oceans

When crystals of salt are mixed with water, the crystals disappear. The crystals have dissolved in the water. The molecules of salt have split up into ions, and the ions mix with the water so they can no longer be seen. Most salts, including bromine salts, dissolve easily in water.

When water washes over rocks, some of the bromine minerals from the rocks dissolve in the water. Since oceans cover nearly three-quarters of Earth, there is a huge area where bromine compounds are washed out of rocks and into the water.

Over a long time, bromine builds up in the oceans. Scientists estimate the oceans contain about 85 ppm bromine. If you scooped up one million droplets of seawater, 85 of them will be droplets of dissolved bromine. The oceans contain

much more bromine than Earth's rocks. But the bromine in the water is still bonded to other elements as compounds.

This salt flat in Bolivia was created when an ancient sea evaporated and left salt behind. Many of the salts are bromine compounds.

Bromine on land

Earth's dry land is not stuck to the surface of the planet. Instead, the land slides very slowly across the surface, moving only a few inches in a year. As the land moves, it may be covered by the ocean or it may lift seabeds up to make shallow seas.

These shallow seas slowly dry out to form new areas of dry land. When an ocean dries, the water evaporates into the air, leaving behind the minerals that were dissolved in the water. The deposits left behind by ancient oceans are good sources of bromine. The deposits are sometimes called brines. In the United States, for example, Arkansas and Michigan have underground brines that contain bromine salts. Bromine is found in these brines at 10,000 ppm, the highest concentration of bromine compounds in the world.

Producing bromine

Some compounds of bromine have been used for thousands of years. In ancient times people did not understand that those substances contained the element bromine, but they took advantage of the element's properties anyway.

For example, three thousand years ago, the Phoenicians, who lived where Lebanon is today, extracted bromine compounds from certain types of clams and snails that lived on the shores of the Mediterranean Sea. The compounds were used to make dyes. One of these dyes, known as "Tyrian purple," was so valuable and expensive to produce that only kings and emperors were rich enough to have all their clothes colored with it. As a result the color of the dye became known as "royal purple." However, the dye was actually a deep red, not purple.

Official discovery

Two scientists, German chemist Carl Löwig (1803–1890) and French chemist Antoine J. Balard (1802–1876), discovered the element bromine at about the same time in 1826. Löwig was a chemistry student and isolated bromine by accident while experimenting with chlorine and seawater. He knew he had found an interesting new substance, but he did not realize it was a new element.

At the same time, Balard was a professor of chemistry looking for new medicinal substances in seawater. He also isolated bromine by accident, but unlike Löwig, Balard realized he had found a new element. Balard was the first to announce his discovery and introduce the element to other scientists.

The Roman emperor Augustus wore a toga colored red by a bromine-containing dye called Tyrian purple.

Today, Balard usually gets the credit for discovering bromine and is best known for this discovery. However, Löwig continued to study bromine and discovered many new bromine compounds.

Producing bromine

About 500 million kilograms of pure bromine (more than a 747 airplane full of passengers) are produced each year. However, this amount is decreasing because the element is being used less.

In the past, most of the bromine produced was added to gasoline and other fuels. However, many countries have banned this type of gasoline because it has been linked to health problems. As a result, pure bromine is not in high demand.

Today, the United States is the largest producer of bromine. Israel, Great Britain, China, and a few other countries also produce small amounts of the element.

The French chemist Antoine J. Balard is credited with discovering bromine in 1826.

Bromine is purified from salts taken from rocks and seawater. In the United States, these bromine compounds come from brine deposits.

Mining salts

Brine is the name used for water that is saturated, or full, of salt. Because many salts include bromine compounds, water full of salt often contains large amounts of bromine. Millions of years ago, the southeastern United States was covered by the ocean. The seabed slowly moved upward, and the ocean dried up. Solid salt

DID YOU KNOW?

Though bromine was discovered in 1826, it was not produced by businesses until many decades later. One reason is that no one had a use for bromine. A second reason is that bromine is not easy to extract from its compounds. In the 1930s American William Dow, the head of the U.S. Dow Chemical Company, was one of the first to extract bromine from seawater in large quantities using electricity.

was left on the land. Over the years this layer of salt was covered by sand, mud, and other minerals. The same salt is now buried deep underground and is mined for its bromine minerals.

Purifying bromine

Bromine is sold most often as salts or other compounds because pure bromine is expensive and difficult to produce. This is because bromine atoms are very reactive and hard to separate from compounds.

Piles of salt are collected at a salt mine. Pure bromine is extracted from the salts.

Pure bromine can be produced by a reaction with chlorine (Cl). Chlorine is more reactive than bromine. When chlorine reacts with a bromide salt, it takes the place of the bromine in the compound. This produces a chloride salt and pure bromine.

Pure chlorine is made by the electrolysis of sodium chloride (NaCl). Electrolysis uses a large electric current to turn the ions in compounds into atoms. (An electric current is formed when electrons travel through a substance in the same direction.) Sodium chloride is table salt, which is used in cooking. It is a very common compound and that makes

Waste bromine vapor is released from a smokestack at a chemical plant in Israel beside the Dead Sea.

chlorine less expensive to purify than bromine. Bromine is sometimes also purified by electrolysis.

Solid sodium bromide salt is heated until it melts. When it melts, the salt splits up into ions. A large electric current is passed through the liquid salt between two points called electrodes. As is flows through the salt, the current takes an electron from each bromide ion (Br^-) to make it a bromine atom. The current also gives an electron to each sodium ion (Na^+) to make them sodium atoms. The pure sodium gathers at one electrode, while pure bromine is formed at the other.

Recycling

Bromine compounds are easy to find but making pure bromine takes a lot of work. In order to recycle the bromine already in use, scientists are studying how to extract bromine from human-made products, such as televisions and electronic equipment. They hope that recycled bromine will be easier and less expensive to produce than bromine purified from minerals. Recycling will also stop the bromine compounds in garbage from polluting the environment.

Chemistry and compounds

Bromine reacts with aluminum to form aluminum bromide. That compound forms yellow crystals, and the reaction produces a lot of heat and flames.

Bromine, like all of the halogens, is a highly reactive element. All halogens have seven electrons in their outermost electron shell. They need only one more electron to become stable. This arrangement of electrons is the key to how bromine atoms form bonds.

Attracting electrons

The nucleus of an atom is positively charged because of the protons in it. The positive charge attracts the negative charge of the electrons around the nucleus. This force keeps the electrons in orbit and holds the atom together.

The nuclei of some atoms hold on to electrons more strongly than others. Atoms that need only one electron to fill their outer shell have a stronger pull on their own electrons and the electrons of other atoms. So bromine atoms pull on electrons more strongly than the atoms of elements that need two or three electrons to become stable. This strong pull on electrons is what makes bromine atoms take part in chemical reactions so easily.

Some elements, such as sodium, have only one electron in their atom's outer shell. A sodium atom becomes stable by losing that single outer electron. As a result, the sodium atom holds onto the outer electron only very weakly.

When a sodium atom meets a bromine atom they react. During the reaction, the bromine atom pulls the outer electron from the sodium. The two atoms then become a pair of ions—Na^+ and Br^-. The ions attract each other and bond to form sodium bromide.

Changes in reactivity

Despite being more reactive than most elements, bromine is not the most reactive member of the halogens.

Halogens with smaller atoms, such as fluorine, are more reactive than those with larger ones, such as astatine. The outer electrons of a smaller atom are closer to the nucleus than those of a larger atom. As a result, the electrons are pulled toward the nucleus more strongly in smaller atoms. Inside larger atoms the outer electrons are held in place less firmly by the nucleus because they are farther away from it.

Halogens react by pulling electrons from other atoms into their outer shells. The halogen with the strongest pull will be the most reactive. Fluorine is the halogen with the smallest atoms and pulls on electrons more strongly than any other halogen. It is the most reactive of all the nonmetal elements.

Chlorine atoms are the next smallest, so chlorine is the second-most reactive halogen. Bromine is third most reactive, followed by iodine and astatine. Iodine atoms are larger than those of bromine, so it is less reactive. Astatine is the least reactive halogen because it has the largest atoms. As a result, astatine atoms form compounds less easily.

Bromine is the only liquid halogen at room temperature. Chlorine is a pale green gas, and iodine is a dark gray solid.

Chlorine

Bromine

Iodine

ATOMS AT WORK

When potassium iodide (KI) and bromine (Br$_2$) are mixed together, a displacement reaction takes place. The bromine takes the place of iodine in the compound.

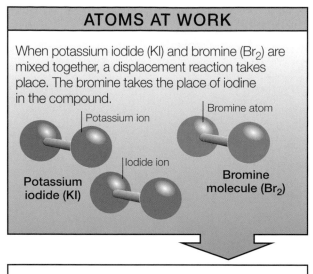

Potassium ion

Bromine atom

Iodide ion

Potassium iodide (KI)

Bromine molecule (Br$_2$)

Each bromine atom pulls an electron from an iodide ion. The bromine becomes an ion while the iodide becomes an atom.

Electron

Bromide ion

Iodine atom

Potassium

Iodide ion

Bromine atom

The bromide ion is attracted to a potassium ion and forms a potassium bromide (KBr) molecule. The iodine atoms bond into an iodine molecule (I$_2$).

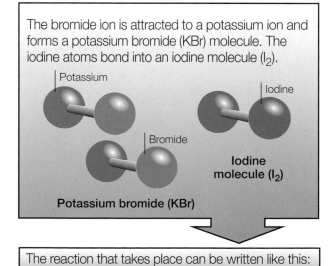

Potassium

Iodine

Bromide

Iodine molecule (I$_2$)

Potassium bromide (KBr)

The reaction that takes place can be written like this:

2KI + Br$_2$ → 2KBr + I$_2$

Displacement reactions

The differences in reactivity among the halogens can be seen in reactions called displacement reactions. In a displacement reaction, one atom takes the place of another atom in a compound.

For example, if bromine (Br$_2$) was mixed with potassium iodide (KI), the bromine atoms would displace the iodide ions to form potassium bromide and pure iodine. In this case, bromine has smaller, more reactive atoms than iodine. The bromine atom (Br) takes the electron from the iodide ion (I$^-$). The bromine becomes a bromide ion (Br$^-$), and the iodide ion becomes an uncharged iodine atom (I). The bromide ion bonds with the potassium ion (K$^+$) to form potassium bromide.

If chlorine was added to the bromide compound, it would displace the bromine in the same way. This is the reaction often used to make pure bromine.

Bromocarbons

Organic compounds all contain carbon. Most of them also have at least some hydrogen atoms. The simplest organic compound of all is methane (CH$_4$). Carbon atoms can form into long chains, rings, and other complicated shapes. That makes it possible for many millions of organic compounds to exist. Organic compounds occur in substances such as petroleum oil, coal, and natural gas.

Organic compounds that contain bromine are called bromocarbons. One of the simplest bromocarbons is bromomethane (CH_3Br). This gas is used to kill pests, such as rodents, rabbits, and worms. Adding one more bromine atom makes dibromomethane (CH_2Br_2). The word *di* is used in chemistry to mean "two." Another bromocarbon is bromoethane (C_2H_5Br). It is used in the chemical processes that make plastics and medicines.

Covalent bonds

Bromine atoms bond to carbon atoms to form bromocarbons. The atoms do not form ions but bond by sharing electrons instead. Bonds in which atoms share electrons are covalent. When two atoms share a pair of electrons, each electron is being pulled in two directions, toward the nuclei of both atoms. These forces are what keep the atoms bonded together.

A carbon atom has four outer electrons. Carbon always forms bonds by sharing electrons with other atoms. It must share four more electrons to become stable. A carbon atom will share one electron with a bromine atom. That bromine atom now has a full set of eight electrons, while the carbon has five electrons. In bromomethane, the carbon atom is sharing electrons with one bromine atom and three hydrogen atoms. All the atoms in the compound have full outer shells and are stable.

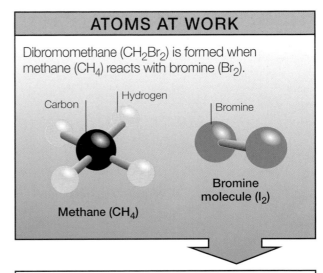

ATOMS AT WORK

Dibromomethane (CH_2Br_2) is formed when methane (CH_4) reacts with bromine (Br_2).

Carbon · Hydrogen · Bromine

Bromine molecule (I_2)

Methane (CH_4)

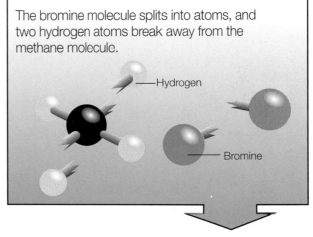

The bromine molecule splits into atoms, and two hydrogen atoms break away from the methane molecule.

Hydrogen

Bromine

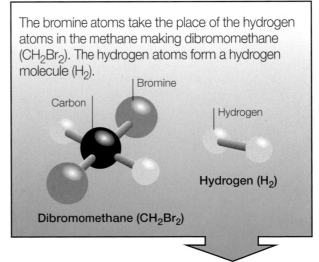

The bromine atoms take the place of the hydrogen atoms in the methane making dibromomethane (CH_2Br_2). The hydrogen atoms form a hydrogen molecule (H_2).

Bromine

Carbon

Hydrogen

Hydrogen (H_2)

Dibromomethane (CH_2Br_2)

The reaction that takes place can be written like this:
$CH_4 + Br_2 \rightarrow CH_2Br_2 + H_2$

How bromine is used

Bromine is highly reactive and can be used to make a wide range of compounds. Many of these compounds have been used by people in the past. However, today bromine is used less because it is very poisonous.

Previous uses

In the past, the most common bromine compound used was dibromoethane ($C_2H_4Br_2$). This was added to gasoline along with lead compounds as an "antiknock" agent for car engines. The purpose of the lead was to help the gasoline burn evenly in the engine. Without it, the gasoline would burn too fast, causing jerks, or knocks, inside the engine. After the fuel burned, the lead reacted with the dibromoethane to form a gas that could be swept out of the engine in the exhaust.

By the 1970s, governments began phasing out leaded gasoline because of concerns about its harmful effects on health.

Cars more than thirty years old run on gasoline containing bromine compounds. Modern engines are designed to use less-poisonous fuel.

A photograph is developed in a dark room. Photographic paper and film is covered in silver bromide, which is sensitive to light.

By the 1990s leaded gasoline was banned in most countries. Unleaded gasoline does not contain dibromoethane. That greatly reduced the amount of bromine needed by industries.

Photographic film

Bromide was used in much smaller amounts in photographic film. This film was used before digital cameras were invented. The film is a strip of plastic coated with silver bromide. The silver bromide compound is sensitive to light. When the film is exposed to light, the bromine atoms are removed, leaving tiny silver crystals to form an image on the film.

Some photographers still use film in their cameras. However, most people use digital cameras and print their pictures using a computer. As a result, only a little bromine is needed for films.

Fireproofing

Today, half of the bromine produced is used in fire retardants. Fire retardants can stop things from bursting into flames or can make them burn slowly. There are many different types of fire retardants that contain bromine. Together, these compounds are known as brominated fire retardants (BFRs).

BFRs are added to many electronic products to make them more resistant to fire. Televisions, computers, and cell phones

Inspectors check the cushions of airplane seats that have been burned. The cushions are coated with BFRs to stop them from bursting into flames.

ATOMS AT WORK

Brominated fire retardants (BFRs) work by robbing the air of the oxygen needed for a fire to burn. BFRs contain bromine atoms.

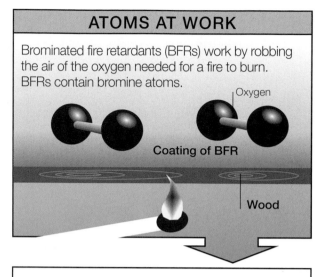

When the substance containing the BFR heats up, the bromine atoms are released into the air, where they react with oxygen atoms.

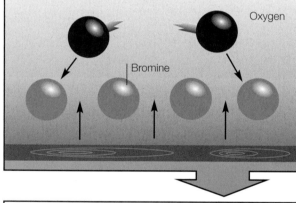

The bromine and oxygen atoms form dibromine monoxide (Br_2O).

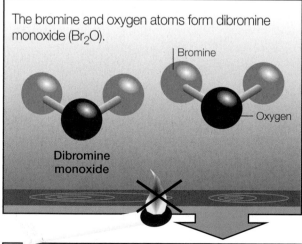

When the oxygen is taken from the air, there is no oxygen available for a fire to start or continue to burn.

all contain BFRs. Items such as children's clothing and some camping equipment contain BFRs, too.

Blocking oxygen

Burning is usually caused when a substance begins to react with oxygen (O_2) in the air. The BFRs prevent fires by taking away the oxygen needed for a fire to burn.

When something containing a BFR gets really hot, it releases bromine atoms into the air. The bromine atoms quickly form bonds with the oxygen in the air. The bromine ties up the oxygen so there is not enough for a fire to start.

Killing pests

Most of the other products containing bromine compounds are used to kill pests, such as insects. Tiny amounts of bromine are also added to water to kill any bacteria that might cause diseases. Bromine is used in certain cleaners and bleaches, along with chlorine.

The future

The future of bromine use is hard to predict. Some experts suggest current usage will go down as even more safer non-bromine compounds are developed. Scientists are currently testing bromine in batteries used to power electric cars. Some new medicines may also contain bromine.

Bromine and health

Pure bromine is a serious health hazard to humans. As a gas it can burn the eyes, throat, and lungs. As a liquid spilled on the skin it produces painful blisters and burns. If swallowed, bromine can damage the nerves and brain. The element is very poisonous and is only handled with proper safety equipment.

Bromine in the body

In recent years, scientists have learned that some of the bromine compounds added to everyday products get into some foods. People eat the food, and bromine builds up in the body. For example, studies have shown high levels of bromine in human fat, and in some of the fish we eat.

One type of bromine compound, called a 6 diphenyl ether (PBDE), appears to be building up in people living in the United States. PBDEs are used in electronic equipment and furniture. The United States is the world's largest producer of PBDEs. Americans have ten to twenty times more PBDEs in the body than people who live in Europe. Europeans have double the amount of PBDEs than people in Japan. Some research suggests the amount of PBDEs in humans is still going up, doubling every four to five years. That is because greater amounts of PBDEs are being produced.

However, there is no connection between high levels of PBDEs in the body and bad health. Scientists believe the levels of PBDEs detected in humans and foods are still not high enough to do any damage.

This bottle of pure bromine has labels warning how dangerous the element is. Liquid bromine burns the skin and bromine vapor damages the lungs.

25

PBDEs are used in all electronics, such as this circuit board, to make them fireproof.

Bromine in the environment

Once bromine compounds get into the air, water, and soil, they do not go away easily. Scientists call this a persistent compound, because it persists (lasts) in the environment for long periods of time. This is because bromine compounds are very stable. Once they form, they are unlikely to react again and turn into other substances. The bonds in bromine compounds are very strong and can only be broken using large amounts of energy. In nature, bromine bonds form easily, but they break only on rare occasions. For example, bromine compounds were being used as pesticides on crops. That was

A researcher tests a sample of PBDE to check whether it is harmful to health.

stopped when concerns over health effects became known. Nearly twenty years later, bromine compounds were still in the soil.

A genetic fingerprint is revealed by a series of pink lines that glow in certain light. The lines show what genes a person has. The pink color comes from a dye called bromine ethidium.

Controlling bromine

Concerns over persistent bromine compounds building up in the environment are causing some governments and companies to take action. The European Union (EU) banned the use of two types of common PBDEs in 2004 and is working to lower levels of other compounds in the environment. The EU has suggested it is likely PBDEs could cause harm to humans, and banned them before they could damage health.

Many of the world's largest companies have stopped adding PBDEs to the products they manufacture. Many of the latest computers and electronic items no longer contain these substances. PBDEs are also no longer used to make many types of furniture.

DID YOU KNOW?

In order to learn how PBDEs can affect health, scientists have studied the effect of PBDEs on the development of baby rats. Pregnant rats were injected with PBDEs, and their babies were watched closely. As the babies grew, some organs did not develop correctly. Female rats grew abnormal reproductive organs. Some of the other organs in male rats were also small, including those used by the immune system.

Periodic table

Everything in the universe is made from combinations of substances called elements. Elements are made of tiny atoms, which are the building blocks of matter.

The characteristics of an atom depends on how many tiny particles called protons are located in its center, or nucleus. An element's atomic number is the same as the number of its protons.

Scientists have found around 116 different elements. About 90 elements occur naturally on Earth. The rest have been made in experiments.

All these elements are set out on a chart called the periodic table. This lists all the elements in order according to their atomic number.

The elements on the left side of the table are metals. Those at the right are nonmetals. Between the metals and the nonmetals are the metalloids, which sometimes act like metals and sometimes act like nonmetals.

● On the left of the table are the alkali metals. These have just one outer electron.

● Metals get more reactive as you go down a group. The most reactive nonmetals are at the top of the table.

● On the right of the periodic table are the noble gases. These elements have full outer shells.

● The number of electrons orbiting the nucleus increases as you go down each group.

● Elements in the same group have the same number of electrons in their outer shells.

● The transition metals are in the middle of the table, between Groups II and III.

Group I

Group II

Transition metals

1 H Hydrogen 1								
3 Li Lithium 7	4 Be Beryllium 9							
11 Na Sodium 23	12 Mg Magnesium 24							
19 K Potassium 39	20 Ca Calcium 40	21 Sc Scandium 45	22 Ti Titanium 48	23 V Vanadium 51	24 Cr Chromium 52	25 Mn Manganese 55	26 Fe Iron 56	27 Co Cobalt 59
37 Rb Rubidium 85	38 Sr Strontium 88	39 Y Yttrium 89	40 Zr Zirconium 91	41 Nb Niobium 93	42 Mo Molybdenum 96	43 Tc Technetium (98)	44 Ru Ruthenium 101	45 Rh Rhodium 103
55 Cs Cesium 133	56 Ba Barium 137	71 Lu Lutetium 175	72 Hf Hafnium 179	73 Ta Tantalum 181	74 W Tungsten 184	75 Re Rhenium 186	76 Os Osmium 190	77 Ir Iridium 192
87 Fr Francium 223	88 Ra Radium 226	103 Lr Lawrencium (260)	104 Rf Rutherfordium (263)	105 Db Dubnium (268)	106 Sg Seaborgium (266)	107 Bh Bohrium (272)	108 Hs Hassium (277)	109 Mt Meitnerium (276)

Lanthanide elements

Actinide elements

57 La Lanthanum 39	58 Ce Cerium 140	59 Pr Praseodymium 141	60 Nd Neodymium 144	61 Pm Promethium (145)
89 Ac Actinium 227	90 Th Thorium 232	91 Pa Protactinium 231	92 U Uranium 238	93 Np Neptunium (237)

The horizontal rows are called periods. As you go across a period, the atomic number increases by one from each element to the next. The vertical columns are called groups. Elements get heavier as you go down a group. All the elements in a group have the same number of electrons in their outer shells. This means they react in similar ways.

The transition metals fall between Groups II and III. Their electron shells fill up in an unusual way. The lanthanide elements and the actinide elements are set apart from the main table to make it easier to read. All the lanthanide elements and the actinide elements are quite rare.

Bromine in the table

Bromine belongs to Group VII, or seven, in the table. This group is known as the halogens. Bromine is the only halogen that is liquid in normal conditions. As with all halogens, bromine has seven electrons in the outer shell. It needs one electron to become stable. Most of bromine's reactions are with metals that have electrons to give away.

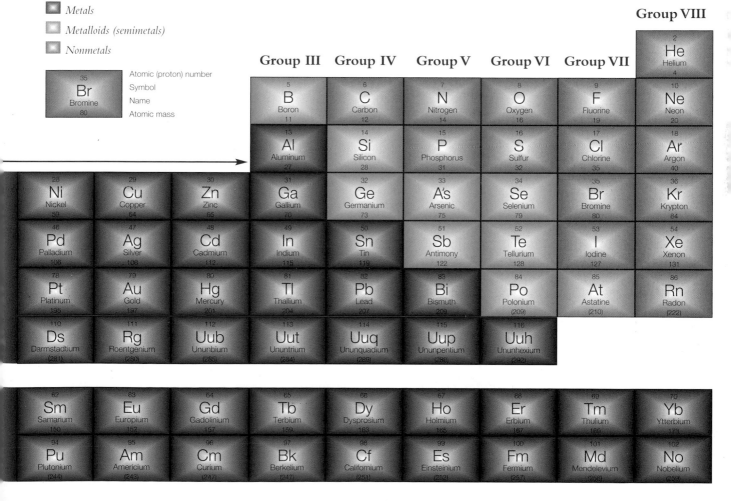

Chemical reactions

Chemical reactions are going on all the time. Some reactions involve just two substances, while others involve many more. Whenever a reaction takes place, at least one substance is changed.

In a reaction, the number and type of atoms stay the same. But they join up in different combinations to form new molecules.

Pure bromine is produced when chlorine gas is bubbled through potassium bromide. The chlorine replaces the bromine in the compound, making potassium chloride and pure bromine, which is seen here as a yellow liquid.

ATOMS AT WORK

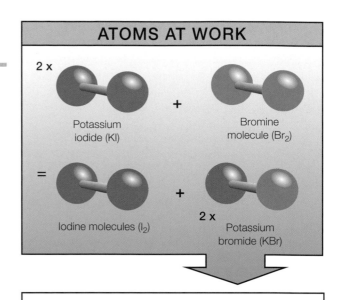

2 x Potassium iodide (KI) + Bromine molecule (Br$_2$)

= Iodine molecules (I$_2$) + 2 x Potassium bromide (KBr)

The reaction that take place when bromine reacts with potassium iodide is written like this:

$$2KI + Br_2 \rightarrow I_2 + 2KBr$$

This tells us that two molecules of potassium iodide react with one bromine molecule to form one molecule of iodine and two molecules of potassium bromide.

Writing an equation

Chemical reactions can be described by writing down the arrangement of the atoms involved before the reaction and their arrangement after the reaction. The number of atoms will be the same at the beginning and end of the reaction. Chemists write the reaction as a chemical equation.

When the numbers of each atom on both sides of the equation are equal, the equation is balanced. If the numbers are not equal, something is wrong. The chemist adjusts the number of atoms involved until the equation balances.

Glossary

atom: The smallest part of an element having all the properties of that element. Each atom is less than a millionth of an inch in diameter.

atomic mass number: The number of protons and neutrons in an atom.

atomic number: The number of protons in an atom.

bond: The sharing or exchanging of electrons between atoms that holds them together to form molecules.

brine: Water with a large amount of salt dissolved in it, or a soft rock made up of salt crystals.

compound: A substance made of atoms of more than one element. The atoms are held together by chemical bonds.

crystal: A solid consisting of a repeating pattern of atoms, ions, or molecules.

electrode: A material through which an electrical current flows into, or out of, another substance.

electrolysis: The use of electricity to change a substance chemically.

electron: A tiny particle with a negative charge. Electrons are found inside atoms, where they move around the nucleus in layers called electron shells.

element: A substance that is made from only one type of atom. Bromine belongs to a group of elements called the halogens.

equation: A way of using numbers and symbols to explain how a chemical reaction takes place.

halogen: A type of element with atoms containing seven electrons in their outer shells. Bromine is a halogen.

ion: An atom or a group of atoms that has lost or gained electrons to become electrically charged.

isotopes: Atoms of an element with the same number of protons and electrons but different numbers of neutrons.

mineral: A compound or element as it is found in its natural form on Earth.

neutron: A tiny particle with no electrical charge. Neutrons are found in the nucleus of almost every atom.

nonmetal: An element on the right-hand side of the periodic table.

nucleus: The dense structure at the center of an atom. Protons and neutrons are found inside the nucleus of an atom.

periodic table: A chart containing all the chemical elements laid out in order of their atomic number.

proton: A tiny particle with a positive charge. Protons are found inside the nucleus of an atom.

radioactivity: The release of energy and particles caused by changes in the nucleus of an unstable atom.

reaction: A process in which two or more elements or compounds combine to produce new substances.

Index